LAMAR JACKSON

THE BOY WHO BECAME A STAR QUARTERBACK

This book belongs to

_____

CONTENTS

Chapter 1: Early Years

Chapter 2: College Years

Chapter 3: NFL Draft and Rookie Season

Chapter 4: First MVP

Chapter 5: Overcoming Obstacles

Chapter 6: Second MVP

Chapter 7: Playing Style

Chapter 8: Lessons and Inspirations

CHAPTER 1

Early Years

Lamar Demeatrice Jackson Jr. was born on January 7, 1997, to Felicia Jones and Lamar Jackson Sr. in Pompano Beach, Florida. Growing up in a neighborhood that faced economic challenges, Lamar experienced loss at a young age when his father passed away from a heart attack on the same day his grandmother died. At just 8 years old, Lamar, along with his younger brother and two sisters, was raised by his mother.

Despite the hardships, Lamar found joy and passion in playing football. He attended public schools and joined the Pop Warner football league, where he first showcased his talent. Even at the age of 8, Lamar displayed his impressive arm strength, throwing a football 20 yards.

Lamar's journey to football stardom began to take shape in high school. Although he started his high school football career relatively late, not joining a team until his junior year, Lamar quickly made a name for himself. He attended Santaluces High School before transferring to Boynton Beach High School in Boynton Beach, Florida.

At Boynton Beach High, Lamar excelled as a read-option quarterback, showcasing both his running and passing skills. Over two years, Lamar threw for over 2,000 yards and 31 touchdowns, while also rushing for over 1,600 yards and 22 touchdowns. One of his memorable plays, where he juked past defenders and strutted into the end zone, even went viral online!

Despite his young age, Lamar possessed determination and drive beyond his years. He knew that achieving his dreams would take hard work and dedication, but he was willing to put in the effort. He had a fire burning inside him – a burning desire to succeed.

The road ahead would be filled with challenges and obstacles, but he was ready to face them head-on. With a football in his hand and a dream in his heart, Lamar Jackson's journey was just beginning. And this is the story of how he became a gridiron star.

CHAPTER 2

College Years

After graduating from high school, Lamar Jackson caught the attention of college recruiters across the country. He was highly sought after by both big-name schools like Louisville, Florida, Auburn, and Clemson, as well as mid-major programs like Akron, Western Kentucky, and Marshall.

Lama visited a handful of schools, including Louisville, Florida, Nebraska, and Mississippi State, carefully considering each one. There was even a moment when it seemed like he might sign with Florida, but in the end, Lamar made the decision to commit to the University of Louisville.

One thing that played a big role in Lamar's decision was a promise made by Louisville's head coach, Bobby Petrino. Coach Petrino assured Lamar's mother that her son would have the opportunity to play quarterback and nothing else – a promise that meant a lot to Lamar and his family as they looked ahead to the next chapter of his football journey.

In the first year at the University of Louisville, Lamar Jackson embarked on a thrilling journey as a freshman football player. While balancing his studies as a communications major, Lamar stepped onto the field and showcased his talents in 12 games, starting in eight of them.

Throughout the season, Lamar demonstrated his versatility as a quarterback, completing passes and making plays with his legs. He threw for 1,840 yards and 12 touchdowns while also rushing for an impressive 960 yards and 11 touchdowns. Lamar became known as a dynamic playmaker on the field .

But perhaps the most exciting moment of Lamar's freshman season came in the 2015 Music City Bowl. In this game, Lamar passed for 227 yards and two touchdowns. Additionally, he set a Music City Bowl record by rushing for an incredible 226 yards and two touchdowns. His outstanding performance earned him the title of MVP, cementing his status as a rising star in college football.

As Lamar Jackson entered his sophomore year at the University of Louisville, he continued to amaze fans with his skills. Against powerhouse teams like Florida State and Clemson, Lamar shone brightly, leading Louisville to impressive victories and racking up numerous awards along the way.

On December 10, 2016, Lamar's dreams became a reality when he was awarded the Heisman Trophy, becoming the youngest-ever recipient of the award at just 19 years old. It was a historic moment for Lamar and the University of Louisville, as he became the first player from the school to win the Heisman Trophy.

In the 2017 season, Lamar continued to showcase his talent, earning him a spot as a finalist for the prestigious Heisman Trophy. Although he finished in third place in the Heisman voting, Lamar's exceptional statistics spoke for themselves.

In 13 games, Lamar dazzled fans with his talent, throwing for over 3,600 yards and 27 touchdowns, while also rushing for over 1,600 yards and 18 touchdowns. At the end of the school year, he was honored as the men's ACC Athlete of the Year for all conference sports, a testament to his outstanding athleticism and contributions to the University of Louisville.

CHAPTER 3

NFL Draft and Rookie Season

In January 2018, Lamar announced that he would enter the 2018 NFL draft, a thrilling step forward in his journey.

At the NFL Scouting Combine, where players show off their skills to NFL teams, Lamar made a bold choice. Instead of running drills like the 40-yard dash, which could have highlighted his speed, Lamar chose to focus on showcasing his passing abilities. He wanted to prove to everyone that he had what it takes to be a top-notch quarterback in the NFL.

Lamar Jackson's dream came true when he was drafted by the Baltimore Ravens in the first round. It was a big moment for Lamar and his fans as he embarked on his professional football journey.

Signing his rookie contract on June 5, Lamar was ready to prove himself on the big stage. He made his NFL debut in the season opener against the Buffalo Bills, showing off his skills both passing and running the ball.

Throughout the season, Lamar continued to impress, scoring his first NFL touchdown against the New Orleans Saints and throwing his first touchdown pass to fellow rookie Hayden Hurst. He even set records, like rushing for the most yards by a quarterback in a single game in Ravens franchise history!

When starting quarterback Joe Flacco got injured, Lamar stepped up to the challenge, making his first NFL start against the Cincinnati Bengals. He didn't disappoint, leading the Ravens to victory with his passing and rushing abilities.

As the season went on, Lamar's star continued to rise. He helped the Ravens clinch the AFC North title and led the team to an impressive 6-1 record in the games he started. Lamar's unique skills as a quarterback, both throwing and running the ball, made him a force to be reckoned with on the field.

In his first NFL playoff game, just one day before his 22nd birthday, Lamar showed his resilience and determination, leading a thrilling comeback against the Los Angeles Chargers. Though the Ravens ultimately fell short, Lamar's performance proved that he was ready for the challenges of the NFL.

CHAPTER 4

First MVP

In 2019, Lamar Jackson soared to new heights as he made history on the football field. It was a season filled with incredible moments and unforgettable achievements for the young quarterback.

It all began in the season-opener against the Miami Dolphins, where Lamar put on a show, throwing for a career-high 324 yards and five touchdowns. This outstanding performance made him the youngest quarterback ever to achieve a perfect passer rating in a victory.

As the season progressed, Lamar continued to shine. In Week 2 against the Arizona Cardinals, he rushed for over 100 yards and threw for over 200 yards, setting records and leading the Ravens to victory.

Week after week, Lamar's talent seemed to know no bounds. Against the Cincinnati Bengals, he became the first player in NFL history to pass for over 200 yards and rush for over 150 yards in a regular-season game. And against the Los Angeles Rams, Lamar threw for an impressive five touchdowns, making him the youngest player ever with multiple five-touchdown passing games.

By the end of the season, Lamar's incredible achievements spoke for themselves. He led all quarterbacks in touchdown passes and had the highest passer rating in the league. He also led all rushers with an impressive yards per carry average.

Lamar Jackson's incredible performances earned him the highest honor in the NFL — the Most Valuable Player (MVP) award. It was a historic moment for Lamar, as he joined the ranks of legendary players like Tom Brady and Jim Brown.

Lamar's MVP win was particularly special because he was the second player in history to be voted unanimously for the award. This meant that every voter agreed that Lamar was the most valuable player in the league — a remarkable achievement for the young quarterback.

In addition to his MVP award, Lamar also made history as one of only four African-American quarterbacks to win the prestigious AP MVP award, alongside greats like Patrick Mahomes, Cam Newton, and Steve McNair.

CHAPTER 5

Overcoming Obstacles

In the 2020 season, Lamar Jackson faced both triumphs and challenges as he led the Baltimore Ravens on the football field.

In the season opener against the Browns, Lamar showed off his skills, throwing for 275 yards and three touchdowns in a thrilling victory. His outstanding performance earned him the title of AFC Offensive Player of the Week.

However, Lamar faced some tough opponents throughout the season. In Week 3 against the Chiefs, he encountered difficulties, throwing for a career-low in yards during a tough loss. But Lamar didn't let setbacks hold him back.

Week after week, Lamar continued to shine. In Week 4 against the Washington Football Team, he made history by becoming the fastest player ever to reach 5,000 passing yards and 2,000 rushing yards in NFL history.

In the Wild Card Round of the playoffs, he secured his first career playoff victory against the Titans, showcasing his talent as both a passer and a rusher.

Though the season ultimately ended with a loss to the Buffalo Bills in the Divisional Round, Lamar's resilience and skill throughout the season showed that he was truly a force to be reckoned with on the football field.

In 2021, Lamar Jackson faced a series of ups and downs with the Baltimore Ravens.

At the start of the year, Lamar received exciting news as the Ravens exercised the fifth-year option on his contract, securing his place with the team for the future.

In Week 1 against the Las Vegas Raiders, Lamar showcased his talent, throwing for over 200 yards and rushing for over 80 yards. Despite a tough loss in overtime, Lamar's performance was a bright spot for the team.

In Week 2 against the Kansas City Chiefs, he secured his first win over star quarterback Patrick Mahomes, showcasing his skills as both a passer and a rusher.

In Week 3 against the Detroit Lions, Lamar once again proved his worth, leading the Ravens to a close victory with a thrilling last-second field goal by Justin Tucker.

But perhaps Lamar's most impressive performance came in Week 5 against the Indianapolis Colts. In a historic game, Lamar threw for over 400 yards and four touchdowns, leading the Ravens to a remarkable comeback victory.

Despite facing challenges, including a career-high four interceptions in Week 12, Lamar continued to lead the Ravens with determination and resilience.

Unfortunately, Lamar's season was cut short due to an ankle injury in Week 14 against the Cleveland Browns. Despite this setback, Lamar's talent and leadership earned him a spot in his second Pro Bowl, a testament to his remarkable abilities on the football field.

With his sights set on the future, Lamar remained determined to overcome any obstacles in his path and continue to shine as one of the NFL's brightest stars.

At the start of the 2022 season, Lamar made headlines when he turned down a contract extension, believing in his ability to improve and achieve even greater success.

In Week 2 against the Dolphins, Lamar delivered an outstanding performance, throwing for over 300 yards and rushing for over 100 yards.

Throughout the first month of the season, Lamar led the league in quarterback rating and passing touchdowns, earning him the title of AFC Offensive Player of the Month. His remarkable playmaking abilities helped propel the Ravens to victory after victory.

However, Lamar faced a setback in Week 13 against the Denver Broncos when he suffered a sprained PCL after being sacked. Despite initial hopes for a quick recovery, Lamar was forced to sit out the final five games of the regular season.

Despite missing several games, Lamar's leadership continued to inspire his team as the Ravens secured a spot in the playoffs. However, Lamar was ruled out for the Wild Card Round game against the Bengals, adding another challenge to his season.

CHAPTER 6

Second MVP

In 2023, Lamar Jackson continued to captivate football fans with his electrifying performances on the field.

After some contract negotiations, Lamar signed a historic five-year deal with the Ravens, becoming the highest-paid player in NFL history. This was just the beginning of a season filled with triumphs and records.

As the season began, Lamar led the Ravens to victory in thrilling matchups against tough opponents like the Bengals and Lions. His incredible performances earned him accolades like the AFC Offensive Player of the Week.

Week after week, Lamar continued to amaze fans with his skills on the field. In Week 12, he reached an impressive milestone, joining a select group of quarterbacks in NFL history by achieving 5,000 career rushing yards in the fewest number of games.

In crucial games against top teams like the San Francisco 49ers and the Miami Dolphins, Lamar showed his leadership and talent, securing crucial wins for the Ravens. His stellar play throughout the season led to him being named the NFL MVP for the second time, a remarkable achievement for a player of his age.

In the playoffs, Lamar's determination and skill were on full display. In the Divisional Round against the Houston Texans, he played a pivotal role in leading the Ravens to victory, showcasing his abilities as both a passer and a rusher.

Though the season ended with a tough loss to the Kansas City Chiefs in the AFC Championship Game, Lamar's contributions to the team's success were undeniable. His resilience and talent continued to inspire football fans everywhere, solidifying his place as one of the greatest players in NFL history.

CHAPTER 7

Playing Style

Lamar Jackson is known for his electrifying style of play, earning him the title of the best running quarterback in the NFL. Ever since his rookie season, Lamar's ability to both pass and run with the football has captured the attention of fans and experts alike.

Often compared to the legendary Michael Vick, Lamar's dual-threat skills make him a force to be reckoned with on the field. Under his leadership, the Baltimore Ravens have consistently dominated in rushing yards, showcasing Lamar's talent for leading his team down the field with speed and agility.

In 2019, Lamar and the Ravens made history by breaking the single-season rushing record. Not only that, but Lamar surpassed Michael Vick's record for the most rushing yards by a quarterback in a single season, solidifying his place as one of the greatest running quarterbacks of all time.

In a memorable game against the Miami Dolphins during the 2023 season, Lamar achieved a perfect passer rating, showcasing his growth and skill as a quarterback. With three perfect passer ratings under his belt, Lamar is tied for the second-most in NFL history, proving that he's not just a running quarterback but also a formidable passer on the field.

CHAPTER 8

Lessons and Inspirations

Lamar Jackson's journey is not just about football; it's about resilience, determination, and the pursuit of dreams. Throughout his life, Lamar has learned valuable lessons that can inspire anyone, no matter their age.

From his early days playing football on the streets of Pompano Beach to becoming an NFL superstar, Lamar's story teaches us the importance of perseverance. Despite facing challenges and setbacks along the way, he never gave up on his dream of playing in the NFL. When things get tough, remember Lamar's journey and keep pushing forward.

Lamar's style of play is one-of-a-kind, blending electrifying speed with pinpoint accuracy. He shows us the power of embracing our own unique talents and abilities, even if they're different from others. Whether you're good at sports, art, music, or something else entirely, be proud of what makes you special.

Despite his immense success, Lamar remains humble and grounded. He understands the importance of hard work, dedication, and staying true to oneself. In a world where fame and attention can sometimes go to people's heads, Lamar serves as a reminder to stay humble and appreciate the people and opportunities around us.

As the quarterback of the Baltimore Ravens, Lamar leads by example both on and off the field. He demonstrates the qualities of a true leader: confidence, courage, and integrity. Whether you're leading a team in sports, school, or any other aspect of life, remember to lead with kindness and respect for others.

Perhaps the most important lesson of all is to dream big and never let anyone tell you that your dreams are out of reach. Lamar's journey from a young boy with a football in his hand to an NFL MVP is proof that anything is possible with hard work, determination, and belief in yourself. So, dare to dream big and chase after your dreams with all your heart.

Made in United States
North Haven, CT
07 December 2024